THE STORY OF
WORLD WAR II

This cemetery overlooking Omaha Beach contains the graves of thousands of Americans killed on D-Day.

THE STORY OF WORLD WAR II

by Stewart Graff

illustrated with photographs

E. P. DUTTON NEW YORK

The author's special thanks to his wife, Polly Anne Graff, and to his editor at Dutton, Ann Troy, for their help in shaping this book.

The quotes from two British soldiers on page 51 are from *Tobruk* by Anthony Heckstall-Smith. Copyright © 1959 by Anthony Heckstall-Smith. Reprinted by permission of W. W. Norton & Company, Inc.

The quote from an American soldier on page 75 is from *Our Jungle Road to Tokyo* by Robert L. Eichelberger. Copyright 1950 by Robert L. Eichelberger. Reprinted by permission of The Viking Press.

Graff, Stewart.   The story of World War II.

SUMMARY: Traces the history of World War II from the events causing the war to the final victory of the allied forces.

1. World War, 1939–1945—Campaigns—Juvenile literature.
[1. World War, 1939–1945]   I. Title
D743.7.G7   940.54'2   77-7522   ISBN: 0-525-40355-8

Published in the United States by E. P. Dutton, a Division of Sequoia-Elsevier Publishing Company, Inc., New York Published simultaneously in Canada by Clarke, Irwin & Company Limited, Toronto and Vancouver

Editor: Ann Troy   Designer: Meri Shardin
Printed in the U.S.A.
10   9   8   7   6   5   4

To the memory of Andrew D. McIntosh
and John T. Reardon of the Taft School,
teachers who brought to so many
the excitement of history

Contents

Maps appear on pages 6-7, 24-25, 36-37, and 54.

The Story

This is the story of a great worldwide war. World War II began in September 1939 and lasted until August 1945. It began in Europe. It spread around the world. Soldiers, sailors, and airmen fought each other across many lands and seas and in the skies.

The war also came to people in their homes—in cities and towns and on farms. The war brought hunger and sickness, cruelty and death, and sadness to millions of men, women, and children. It was a time of daring actions, of blood and sweat, a time when people learned they could be brave.

This is the story of that war—World War II.

Nazi banners decorate the houses of Nuremberg as the people greet Adolf Hitler (standing in the first car) at the start of the Nazi party meeting.

1 | Drumbeats of War

The old German city of Nuremberg blazed with color in the late summer sunlight of the year 1938. Tall red banners with black swastikas almost hid the high gabled houses. Crowds of people milled through the narrow streets. Many wore the Nazi brown-shirted uniforms.

The crowds waited quietly. Then there were shouts. "Here he comes!" Arms shot up in the Nazi salute. Adolf Hitler, dictator of the new Germany, had arrived. The cheers grew into a roar. *"Heil Hitler!"* Hail to Hitler!

Hitler stood in his open car. He raised an arm to answer the salutes. His face was stern, and his eyes looked straight ahead. But the eyes of his followers were the eyes of adoring people. They had found a leader, their Fuehrer—the savior of Germany. Germany had lost the World War of 1914–1918, but Hitler and the Nazis had made their country strong again.

The great yearly rally of the Nazis was beginning in Nuremberg. For a week excitement grew steadily. People heard the cheerful blare of military bands, and march-

3

Above, Germans march in formation in the Nuremberg arena, carrying the Nazi swastika flag. *Below,* Hitler parades through the arena at the climax of the Nazi party yearly rally.

ing boots beat time to the music. Crowds watched mock war games. Torchlight parades lighted the streets at night. Bright searchlights made a dome of light in the night sky. The brilliant flags waved in the breeze. Louder and louder the crowds shouted, *"Heil Hitler!"*

Thousands of people filled the huge Nuremberg hall to hear Hitler's speech. His voice rose to a shout. It sank to a whisper. He thundered of the wrongs done to Germans. He promised that Germany would right those wrongs.

"We did not lose the World War!" Hitler shouted. "We were betrayed by Jews and Communists. They are enemies of the German People. The German People are strong again. We will right the wrongs that were done to us twenty years ago in 1918."

Hitler's voice crackled over the radio across Germany. Most Germans believed him, but there were some who did not. Adolf Hitler had fought his way to power in Germany. His street gangs had beaten down the people who were against him. Thousands of these Germans had been put in prisons called concentration camps. They were helpless, half-starved prisoners. Many were beaten and tortured. Many were worked to death.

The radio carried Hitler's voice across Europe. The small and weak countries around Germany listened. They knew the strength of the German army, and they were afraid.

The leaders in the three great countries of Russia, England, and France listened and worried. The huge Russian nation was east of Germany, beyond the country of Poland. France was next to Germany on the west. Across the waters of the narrow English Channel was England. All three countries feared war.

NORWAY

SWEDEN

NORTH

SEA

DENMARK

ENGLAND

London

HOLLAND

Berlin

Dunkirk

BELGIUM

ENGLISH   CHANNEL

GERMANY

ATLANTIC

NORMANDY

Bastogne

OCEAN

Paris

CZECH

Nuremberg

FRANCE

AUSTRIA

SWITZERLAND

PORTUGAL

SPAIN

ITALY

ADRIATIC   SEA

MEDITERRANEAN   SEA

N

Europe
1939

0   200   400   600

MILES

FINLAND

Leningrad

BALTIC SEA

POLAND

Moscow

RUSSIA

Stalingrad

OVAKIA

HUNGARY

RUMANIA

YUGOSLAVIA

BULGARIA

BLACK SEA

GREECE

TURKEY

Map by George Buctel

Smashed windows in a Jewish shop in Berlin reflect the beginning of Nazi persecution of the Jews.

But Hitler's words were welcome in one big country south of Germany. That country was Italy. Germany and Italy were allies. People called them the Axis powers.

The Nuremberg rally ended. The crowds went home to their cities and villages and farms. In their hearts they were sure that the Germans were a master race. Germany would rule Europe and the world.

Hitler's drums of war beat louder. He would destroy the countries and peoples he hated. Most of all he hated the Jews.

In two November nights in 1938 Hitler struck against the Jewish people of Germany. Hundreds of Jewish homes and apartment houses were burned. Nearly two hundred Jewish synagogues were destroyed. Twenty thousand Jewish men were taken to the concentration camps.

The first country Hitler wanted to attack was Poland. But Hitler was afraid Russia and France and England would all go to war against Germany if he invaded Poland.

Then Hitler received vital news from Joseph Stalin, the Communist dictator of Russia. Stalin would make an agreement with Hitler. Germany could attack Poland. Russia and Germany would not fight each other. Instead they would divide the conquered country. Hitler agreed.

Now Hitler had only France and England to fear. He was ready to risk war with them. He needed only an excuse to strike at Poland.

Hitler called his generals together. "We do not care whether an excuse for war is true," he told them. "It is only victory that counts. Have no pity when you attack."

Hitler made up his excuse. He had a few prisoners taken from one of his prison camps. They were drugged and dressed in Polish army uniforms. He ordered them shot in front of a radio station in a small German town on the Polish border. Then Hitler shouted that Poland had attacked Germany. Pictures of the dead "Polish soldiers" were broadcast to the world. Hitler roared of Germany's revenge against Poland.

A storm of war broke over Europe.

2 | "Have No Pity"

Poland was a large country. Its army had many men but few modern guns. On September 1, 1939, the German air force roared over Poland's airfields and destroyed the Polish air force. German tanks cut through the weak defenses. The German air force bombed cities and towns. The bombs crashed into homes, factories, office buildings, apartment houses, and schools. The bombs blasted them to ruins. Buildings burned. And thousands of men and women, old people and children died.

"Have no pity," Hitler had said.

Then Russia invaded Poland from the east. The Polish armies began to surrender. In just three weeks the country of Poland was only a mass of helpless people. But thousands of her soldiers escaped to France and England. They would fight again.

Germany and Russia divided the conquered country as they had agreed. Polish prisoners of war were put to work in German factories and on German farms.

The Polish cavalry in 1939 before the German and Russian invasions

Many Polish leaders were sent to prison. Many were killed. Neither Hitler nor Stalin had pity.

England and France declared war against Germany. But it was too late to save Poland.

French and British armies gathered in France. They waited for the German attack. The great cities of Paris and London were blacked out at night. Street lights were out. No cars could drive with headlights. People put black curtains over their windows. They feared German bombs from the air. Any light might guide a German bomber plane. Trainloads of children were sent from London into the country to be safe from the bombs.

People waited anxiously. The armies waited. Nothing happened through the winter. The English began to call it the "phony war."

But the war did not stay "phony." Suddenly the Germans attacked. In April 1940 the German army swept

A road in Belgium littered with Belgian army equipment after the country surrendered to the Germans

into Norway to the north. The German march of war rolled on through Denmark and Holland and into Belgium toward France. German planes rained bombs from the sky.

It was a war of sudden terror. People fled. The highways were jammed. No one knew what was happening. Animals crowded the roads. Cows left in the farm fields lowed in pain waiting to be milked. Cars, wagons, wheelbarrows pushed their way along the roads. Crowds of frightened people were trying to escape the Germans.

The German army moved across Belgium ready to attack France. The French rushed soldiers, tanks, and guns to meet the enemy. England sent soldiers, fighting planes, and ships to help her ally, France.

But the Germans moved swiftly around the defending armies. The Germans forced the French and English back to the town of Dunkirk on the shore of the English

In the greatest retreat in history, British and French forces wait to cross the English Channel from Dunkirk, France.

Channel. English guns ringed the town to fight off the German tanks. The British and French were caught in a trap.

In England people sat by their radios and heard the grim news. Over and over the British navy flashed out an order on the radio: "Let every man who can handle a boat sail for Dunkirk."

And the British people came across the water to Dunkirk to rescue their army. They came in yachts, in little boats, in freighters, in navy ships, in fishing boats. They came by anything that had an engine or could sail. Back and forth the boats crossed the twenty-four miles of channel between Dunkirk and England. They came again and again to the beach and docks of Dunkirk. They came to the long, long lines of waiting men.

The German air force attacked. It bombed the British ships and tried to machine-gun the men on the open

German troops march into Paris after the French surrender.

beach. English fighter planes battled savagely to fight off the German planes. The men on the beach waded and swam to the boats. They carried their wounded. By the hundreds and the thousands the men came off the beach and from the docks.

In eight days 370,000 British and French soldiers crossed the English Channel from Dunkirk to England. The English people had brought the men of their army back from France. And thousands of French soldiers had come with them. The French too would fight again.

The men had returned, but their artillery and machine guns and tanks had been left behind. England faced invasion. Italy declared war against France and England. England and France seemed defeated and lost.

The Germans moved quickly to capture the rest of the French armies. German troops marched in victory down the boulevards of Paris. France surrendered.

But England had a new leader, Winston Churchill. "I have nothing to offer but blood, toil, tears, and sweat," he told the nation.

Churchill's strong voice gave his country fresh courage. He called to England's fighting spirit. His words sounded across the land. "We shall fight on the beaches; we shall fight in the fields and in the streets; we shall fight in the hills; we shall never surrender."

The people rallied. The words of the song, "There'll always be an England, and England will be free," rang out in the music halls. The Home Guard practiced with old shotguns. Barbed wire was strung on the beaches. The navy patrolled the Channel. Soldiers drilled with what guns they had.

All England waited.

Across the Channel the Germans planned their attack.

3 | "We Shall Fight"

Hitler's army massed on the shore of northern France. Ships and barges were ready to carry German troops and tanks across the Channel to invade England. The Germans named the plan Operation Sea Lion.

Only some twenty miles of water separated Hitler's army from England at the narrowest point of the Channel—only twenty miles of water between his army and certain victory, if Sea Lion could succeed.

Hitler was sure his navy and air force together would protect Sea Lion against the British navy. But the fighter planes of Britain's Royal Air Force (the RAF) barred the way against the German planes. Before the Germans could invade England, they would have to shoot down Britain's fighter planes and destroy the RAF's airfields.

Field Marshal Hermann Goering commanded the German air force (the Luftwaffe). He had brave pilots, trained to win. "We can destroy England's Fighter Command in four days," Goering promised Hitler.

Air Chief Marshal Hugh Dowding commanded England's RAF Fighter Command. He knew that Germany's planes and pilots outnumbered England's two to one.

Only the RAF's fighter pilots could stop Sea Lion. Most of the pilots were young men. They had taken time from their jobs to train as RAF pilots. They had been well trained. They were daring. They were not fighting to conquer another country. They were fighting to save their own. And they had help from other countries. One of every ten RAF pilots was a Polish air force pilot who had escaped to England.

On August 12, 1940, Goering sent his first wave of bombers and fighter planes against the airfields of the RAF. Dowding had a chain of radar stations that told him when enemy planes were coming near. British fighter planes raced out to fight back the Germans.

Day after day the battles raged. German bombers tried to reach the RAF's airfields. German fighter planes flew with them to protect them from the RAF fighters and to destroy the RAF fighter planes.

Within two weeks the German Luftwaffe had lost 600 planes. The British had lost 300.

Hour after hour the German planes attacked. RAF pilots fought until their fuel ran low. They landed, refueled, and went back to fight again. They snatched a few hours' sleep, and fought again. By September 7 the Luftwaffe seemed sure of victory. One of every four RAF pilots was dead or wounded or missing. The English had only a few reserve planes and pilots left.

On September 7, British radar sounded a new alarm. Four hundred German bombers and 600 fighter planes were coming against England. The RAF's tired, battered fighters braced to meet them. Then came what Marshal

A British radar station

Dowding called a miracle. The German planes did not attack the airfields. Instead they flew on to bomb London. The RAF helped to defend London, but Dowding had enough time to let most of his pilots rest. He repaired the airfields and the radar stations.

The Germans tried once again to destroy the English Fighter Command. Once more the smaller RAF force fought them back. Hitler saw at last that he could not win against the British air force. He knew the Germans could not invade England. Operation Sea Lion was dead.

Winston Churchill's tribute to the RAF fighter pilots will always be remembered. "Never in the field of human conflict was so much owed by so many to so few."

A group of RAF pilots. Churchill said of them, "Never in the field of human conflict was so much owed by so many to so few."

The German air attack on England was not yet over. "Destroy London," Hitler ordered. Through the fall of 1940 and the winter of 1941 the Luftwaffe's bomber planes droned over London night after night. In the darkness the RAF's fighter planes could not help to defend the city. The Germans bombed docks and railways, buildings and homes. People kept buckets of water and sand in their houses to help put out fires from the bombs.

The German bombers flew in like huge night birds. The air-raid sirens howled. People took refuge from the bombs wherever they could. They went to the cellars of their houses, or to special shelters they had built in their back yards. Thousands of families left their homes

St. Paul's Cathedral, in the heart of London, after one of the many German bombing raids.

to sleep in the cold subway stations, deep underground.

Out of the night darkness came the drone of the bombers' engines and then the crash and flames of the bombs. Powerful searchlights pointed through the darkness to find the bombers. The clatter of anti-aircraft gunfire cut through the night.

Weeks and months went on. London's suffering under the bombs seemed endless. But London's people never lost courage.

The King and Queen of England and Winston Churchill often walked the streets where the raids had hit hardest. "Just seeing them made us know we are a country standing together," one man said. And people remembered Churchill's words that called to the fighting spirit of Britain.

The bombings went on until June of 1941. Then the last of the big raids ended. Hitler knew he could not invade England. He knew he could not destroy her by air. He knew he could not break the spirit of the English people. He had lost the Battle of Britain.

Hitler still had one great weapon to use against England. He could try to weaken and starve her. His submarines moved unseen and unheard beneath the surface of the ocean. They launched their torpedoes without warning. They sank ships bringing food and guns and supplies to England. Without those supplies Britain would starve.

German shipyards rang with noise as new submarines were built. The German navy's quiet killers moved out to sea.

4 | The Rolling Tanks

Hitler's maps showed him good news in the winter of 1941. The smaller countries of Hungary, Bulgaria, and Rumania had surrendered to Germany. Rumania's oil wells and refineries supplied oil and gasoline for Germany's tanks and planes. Britain, Germany's enemy to the west, was fighting for her life. German submarines were sinking hundreds of British ships.

Hitler studied one special map again and again. The map showed the huge country of Russia to the east of Germany. Russia's flat plains stretched more than a thousand miles from the great Russian city of Leningrad in the north to the Black Sea in the south. The plains spread five hundred miles from the German border to Russia's capital, Moscow. In summer the plains would be one long, easy highway for Nazi tanks.

If Hitler could conquer Russia, Germany would be the most powerful country in the world. Hitler's spies reported that Russia's armies were not ready for war. Hitler and his generals made their plans. They would attack suddenly. They would split the Russian armies and force them to surrender one by one. They would destroy Russia.

Hitler himself gave the final order. "Conquer, terrorize, and kill." He knew the German army was the greatest in history—three million men, and the tanks, the guns, and the planes they needed. Before dawn on the morning of June 22, 1941, the Germans struck like a whirlwind across Russia's long frontier.

In a little army post on the German border a Russian captain woke to the roar of guns. He ran to the telephone and called thirty miles away to the general in command.

"The Germans are attacking," the captain shouted into the telephone.

There was a silence. "Go back to sleep," the general snapped. "It is impossible."

The general banged down the receiver.

The Russian armies fell back before the German fury. The Germans pushed north toward Leningrad. They drove into central Russia toward Moscow. In the south German tanks rolled across the wide, fertile plains of Russia's Ukraine.

The weather was warm. The German armies swept ahead. It was a joyride for the German soldiers. Their tanks rumbled across the summer farmlands. The soldiers stopped to feast on Russian ducks and chickens. Russian soldiers seemed like cattle to be rounded up.

By late August a German army was within ten miles of Leningrad. The Germans came closer and closer to Russia's big industrial cities. The Russians took the heavy machinery out of their factories. Long trains of flatcars and boxcars carried the machinery far to the east across the Ural Mountains. There the Russians worked day and

N

Germany and Russia
1942

Area occupied by German
forces in late 1942

0   200   400   600
MILES

URAL MOUNTAINS

RUSSIA

Volga River

Stalingrad

CASPIAN SEA

CAUCASUS MOUNTAINS

IRAN

Map by George Buctel

German tanks invade the serene Russian countryside in June 1941.

night to put up new factories to make the guns and tanks and planes they needed.

It was Russia's desperate time. By mid-October the Germans were within forty miles of Moscow, Russia's capital. Stalin stayed grimly in his Moscow headquarters. He knew Moscow stood for all of Russia. The city must be held.

The Germans came nearer and nearer to Moscow. But the warm summer ended. The autumn rains began to fall. They turned the Russian land into a swamp of mud. The German tanks and trucks could not move.

By early November the winds grew colder. The ground froze. Once more the German tanks rumbled forward toward Moscow over the hard ground. By late November German advance patrols were only ten miles from Moscow. Then the deadly Russian winter froze the German army to a stop.

Hitler had been sure the war would be over before winter. He had refused to order heavy winter clothing and winter supplies for his troops. But the Germans had not won, and winter had come.

Frozen hands and feet were wounding Hitler's men as surely as Russian bullets. It was bitter cold. When a man without gloves touched a machine gun, his hand froze to the metal. When he jerked his hand away, his skin stayed frozen to the gun. Hitler's tanks and machine guns and rifles did not have enough of the winter oil they needed.

Thousands of miles to the east Russia had another army. It was there to protect her against Japan. Stalin did not know if the Japanese planned to attack Russia. Then Russian spies sent Stalin vital news. Japan would not attack.

Stalin ordered the best troops of the eastern Russian army to Moscow. The soldiers had been trained to fight in the bitterest cold. Troop trains rumbled westward across the long miles. A new army was coming to Russia's defense.

Stalin's maps showed him grim facts. Russia had lost the places that produced most of her iron and coal. Her best lands were in enemy hands. Stalin knew that more than three million of Russia's soldiers had been killed, captured, or wounded.

In the north the people of Leningrad suffered cruelly. Hitler's orders were brutal. The city and its people were to be destroyed. When the siege began, Leningrad had only a small supply of food. Through the long winter thousands of people died. They dropped in the streets. They collapsed at their work. They died in their homes. There was almost no heat and no drinking water. But

Russian soldiers battle the German army throughout the bitterly cold Russian winter.

the city still lived on. A ring of five thousand guns held back the Germans.

The Russian winter was at its coldest, and Stalin knew that winter had stopped the powerful German army. He ordered Russia's armies to attack.

The Russian attack stunned the Germans. The German army retreated from Moscow. Their abandoned tanks, trucks, and guns littered the icy roads for miles. Soldiers who had made the summer joyride across Russia's farmlands lay dead by the thousands, swept by the snow. A Russian camera saw one such soldier, stiff in death. Only his hair moved restlessly in the wind.

Long lines of German prisoners plodded through Moscow on their way to prison camps. The Russians and the world saw that a German army could be beaten.

The German army kept on retreating. Finally they were able to halt and hold a line. But the line was ninety miles west of Moscow.

All along the Russian front from Leningrad to the south the German army lay like an animal half frozen in the snow, unable to move. But spring would bring warmth again. The animal would thaw and come back to life.

The war for Russia was not over.

5 | "Remember Pearl Harbor"

The war had been fought for two years. Nation after nation had surrendered to Germany. Hitler's armies ranged hundreds of miles across Europe. From Berlin he gave orders that ruled the lives of millions of people.

In a flash on December 7, 1941, the war spread around the world.

Nearly four thousand miles across the Pacific Ocean from Hawaii was the ancient island empire of Japan, not far from the coasts of China and Russia. Japan was not vast in size, but her millions of hard-working, disciplined people believed that their Emperor Hirohito was descended from the goddess of the sun. They were willing to die for their divine Emperor and for their country in order to build a great Japanese empire in Asia. But the United States and Great Britain blocked the way.

The morning of December 7 began like any other quiet Sunday in Hawaii. Japan and the United States were at peace. The ships of America's powerful Pacific

The *Arizona* at Pearl Harbor after the Japanese attack on December 7, 1941. She sank with over 1,000 men aboard.

navy lay at anchor at Pearl Harbor. Suddenly, just before eight o'clock in the morning, planes from Japanese aircraft carriers streaked in from the sea. Their bombs rained down. Japan had struck without warning against the United States.

The bombs tore into the American battleships. Within minutes the ships were burning. Black smoke poured up from their flaming oil. A great explosion blasted through the battleship *Arizona*. The bodies of sailors were rocketed through the air. The wounded and the dying struggled in the water. Minutes later the *Arizona* sank. The *West Virginia* plunged to the harbor bottom. The *Oklahoma* turned over on her side. The battered *California* sank into the mud of the harbor. Bombs ripped through the *Nevada* and the *Tennessee*.

Japanese planes roared over Hickam Field, the American army's airfield. They bombed the planes on the ground. Oil storage tanks went up in flames. Airplane hangars crashed into twisted metal. Burning planes stretched the length of the field. A few American planes struggled into the air to fight the Japanese. Anti-aircraft guns fired against the Japanese planes. But the guns could shoot down only a few of Japan's bombers.

The attack went on for two hours. The Japanese planes flew back to their carriers. They left behind them Pearl Harbor's wrecked battleships, the burned bombers of Hickam Field, and nearly four thousand Americans dead or wounded.

But the Japanese had not destroyed the most important ships of all. America's four big aircraft carriers were safely out at sea. Their planes could still fight.

The news of the Japanese attack flashed out over millions of radios in the United States. A wave of shock

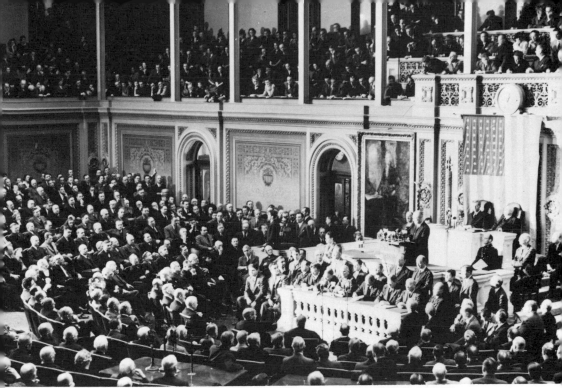

President Roosevelt asks Congress for a declaration of war against Japan.

broke over the country. In one blow half of the American navy had been destroyed or badly damaged.

The next day President Franklin Roosevelt stood before Congress. Across the country people crowded around radios to hear their President. In a solemn voice President Roosevelt called December 7th a "date which will live in infamy." He sounded a call to Americans to fight. Congress declared war against Japan.

Great Britain joined the United States to fight Japan. Germany and Italy were allies of Japan. They declared war against the United States. Hitler's war had become World War II.

Japan had a plan for a vast Asian empire. All the western Pacific Ocean and the lands bordering it were to be Japanese. Only the United States and Great Britain

Thousands of men rush to enlist in the United States army and navy following America's declaration of war. In one month, over 60,000 men enlisted.

could stop her. But now the United States navy could not move, and Great Britain's armies and navy were fighting Germany.

Japan already controlled great parts of China. She had seized the French colony of Indochina (now Vietnam). Her army and navy moved swiftly to the attack. They fortified Japanese islands in the Pacific. They captured the American islands of Wake and Guam. But there were strongholds Japan had still to take. One was the great British fortress of Singapore. Another was the Philippine Islands, where the United States had troops and planes.

The city of Singapore faced the ocean. Its powerful guns pointed out to sea. Hundreds of miles of thick jungle protected it on the land side. Only a few roads cut through the jungle. The British were sure Singapore could fight off any enemy.

The Japanese did not attack by sea. Instead they came by land. Their soldiers walked or rode bicycles over the long miles. They wore sneakers and carried little sacks of rice for food.

The British tried to block the roads. But the Japanese faded into the dark jungle and moved around the British defenses. The Japanese were well trained. They were not afraid of the snakes and insects and the strange noises of the jungle's wild animals at night.

The British retreated. Many of their men were trapped at the road defenses and taken prisoner. They could not stop the Japanese in the tangled jungle. Within weeks the Japanese were outside Singapore.

Singapore's big guns could not be turned around to face the land. They were useless. The city was crowded with people fleeing from the Japanese army. The British fought to hold the Japanese back, but soon there was almost no water or food. The British surrendered. Japan had captured the greatest fortress in southeast Asia.

The Japanese moved on to victory after victory. They took the vast Dutch colony of the East Indies (now Indonesia). They landed an army on the Philippines. They invaded still other parts of China and drove back General Chiang Kai-shek's Chinese army deep into China. They pressed westward into Burma on the edge of India. They went nearly to Australia. Within four months Japan had almost won her empire. Only a corner of the Philippines was left to be conquered.

The corner of the Philippines was the Bataan peninsula. Across from its tip lay the island of Corregidor. American guns on Bataan and Corregidor barred Japa-

The Pacific
1942

Area occupied by Japanese
forces in summer, 1942

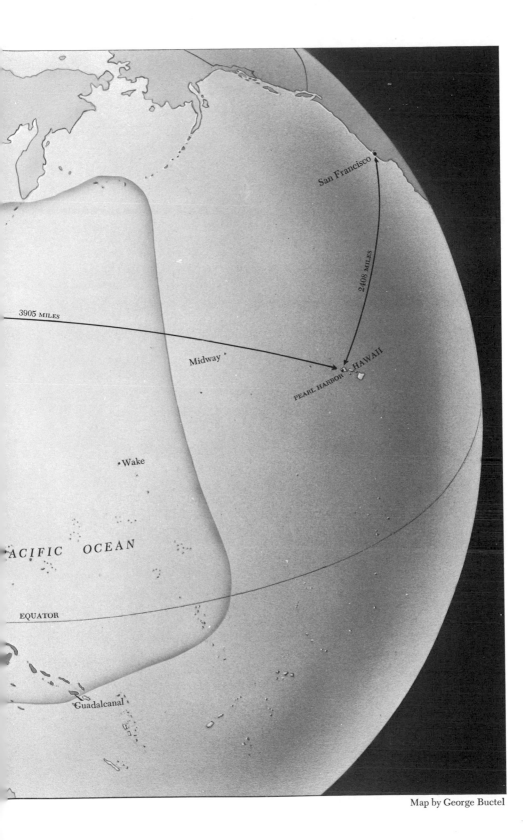

San Francisco

2408 MILES

3905 MILES

Midway

PEARL HARBOR   HAWAII

•Wake

ACIFIC   OCEAN

EQUATOR

Guadalcanal

Map by George Buctel

nese ships from Manila, the capital city of the Philippines. On Bataan was an army of 30,000 United States soldiers and many more soldiers from the Philippines. General Douglas MacArthur was their commander.

The Americans and Filipinos dug in to defend Bataan. Its mountains and jungles and swamps were natural defenses. The soldiers made barriers of thick bamboo sticks, with sharpened points facing the enemy. They strung barbed wire. They dug trenches and foxholes. But Japanese warships and planes controlled the ocean and the air. No help could reach the Americans and Filipinos. They knew it. They said it in a song that began: "We're the battling bastards of Bataan, No mama, no papa, no Uncle Sam. . . ."

General MacArthur was one of America's finest generals. President Roosevelt ordered him to escape to Australia. General Jonathan Wainwright took command. But General MacArthur made a solemn promise: "I shall return."

When the food on Bataan was almost gone, soldiers ate snakes and dogs and jungle monkeys. Thousands of men became weak and sick from lack of food. But the army fought on. Japanese guns blasted the defenses. At last the half-starved Americans and Filipinos surrendered. But before they did, about 2,000 men escaped across the water to the island of Corregidor.

The Japanese rounded up their prisoners. They were taken sixty miles north to prison camps. A few were taken in trucks. The rest had to walk. The men were weak and starving. Many were sick or wounded. They were forced to march hour after hour under a blazing sun. They had little or no food. They were half crazed for water.

Defeated American and Filipino troops are driven at gunpoint by the Japanese during the Death March of Bataan.

Exhausted men collapsed and died where they fell. Sometimes the marching men heard pistol shots behind them. Japanese guards were killing those who had fallen. The marchers knew they must go on or die. The march was a nightmare. Of 75,000 prisoners, almost 10,000 died. It was the Death March of Bataan.

On Corregidor about 11,000 Americans and Filipinos braced themselves for the Japanese attack. Tunnels dug years before in the rock were a shelter. But Japanese shells wrecked the island's big guns and pounded its defenders. The sick and wounded crowded the tunnels. There was almost no food left. The Japanese landed. The fighting was savage, but in the end there was no choice. General Wainwright surrendered Corregidor on May 6, 1942.

An American bomber takes off from the deck of the *Hornet* in a daring raid on Japan.

Japan had won her empire. But across the Pacific Ocean the people of the United States were getting ready to fight a war against both Japan and Germany. "Remember Pearl Harbor" became America's fighting words. Factories and shipyards began to turn out planes and tanks and ships and guns. Young men began their long training as pilots of bombers and fighter planes, and as gunners on the big bombers.

Millions of men were drafted into the army and navy. At railroad stations and bus terminals all over the country men kissed their wives and families and sweethearts goodbye. They went off to a future no one of them could foresee. But behind them the words of a jaunty song echoed, "Don't sit under the apple tree with anyone else but me, 'til I come marching home."*

Even while Japan was going from victory to victory, Americans made a daring raid. The United States aircraft carrier *Hornet* moved secretly toward Japan. The *Hornet* carried sixteen bombers. Seven hundred miles from Japan the bombers took off. They flew in over Japan at treetop level to avoid gunfire. They dropped their bombs on Tokyo and four other cities. Most of the planes were able to fly on to China. The Chinese smuggled the bombers' crews to safety beyond the reach of the Japanese.

The raid told Japan and the world that the United States would strike back at Japan.

6 | The Battle of the Atlantic

The war at sea had begun only two days after Hitler invaded Poland. The British ocean liner *Athenia* was sailing outward bound from England to Canada. A German submarine sent a torpedo crashing into her side without warning. The *Athenia* sank, and more than a hundred people died, some of them Americans.

The German submarine commanders were daring men. They were ready to carry out dangerous, lonely missions. The submarine crews were trained for the days when they were cooped in their small ships. The men were used to long hours below the surface of the sea. They knew there was no escape if depth bombs blasted in the sides of their ships and the ocean water rushed in. England knew her enemy at sea was strong.

A month after the war began, a German submarine made a bold raid. Many British warships were at anchor at their base at Scapa Flow, off the north coast of Scotland. The British believed their ships were safe. But a lone German submarine threaded its way through Scapa

Flow's defenses. Its torpedoes sank the English battle-ship *Royal Oak*. The submarine stole away to safety.

The Germans also had powerful battleships, but the German navy was never as strong as England's. British ships tried to keep the German warships blockaded in Germany's ports.

One big German battleship dashed out to sea as the war began. The *Graf Spee* sailed for the coast of South America. She hunted down British cargo ships, sank them, and disappeared over the horizon. No one knew where she might strike next. Three British warships found the *Graf Spee* at last. The British ships were smaller, but fighting together they were strong. For four-teen hours the guns roared. The *Graf Spee* was cornered. Her commander, Captain Hans Langsdorff, shouted out his orders, and the *Graf Spee* ran for safety into the port of Montevideo in Uruguay. But she found no safety there. Uruguay was not at war. No battleship could stay longer than a few hours.

The *Graf Spee* steamed back to sea off the coast of Argentina. The British ships were waiting. Three hun-dred thousand people lined the shores to see what would happen. Captain Langsdorff knew the British would capture his ship or sink her. If they sank her, most of his crew would die. He acted quickly. He had heavy ex-plosives planted throughout the ship. He put all his crew in lifeboats. The *Graf Spee* blew up in a roaring blast.

Captain Langsdorff led his men safely to Argentina. Three days later he wrapped himself in the flag of the German navy and shot himself. He had followed an an-cient custom of sea captains. He had died with his ship.

The German navy was not England's only enemy at sea. The Italians had swift, strong warships. They lay at

The captain of the German battleship *Graf Spee* evacuated his crew and then blew up the ship rather than surrender her.

anchor in an Italian harbor. British planes made a bold attack. They flew in low, dropped their aerial torpedoes, and soared away. When the attack ended, half the Italian fleet was badly damaged.

Later the British attacked Italian ships at sea. Gunfire flashed all through one night. It was a victory for England. When dawn came, three of Italy's finest ships had been sunk. Others were crippled. The Italian navy never left port again.

Some of the German ships slipped out to sea through the British blockade. One was the great battleship *Bismarck*. British warships and planes pursued her. The *Bismarck* was one of the strongest warships in the world, and she was ready to meet the British. The English attacked. Their shells and torpedoes pounded the *Bis-*

It required both air and sea units of the British navy to sink the powerful German battleship *Bismarck.*

marck's thick sides. They could not destroy her. But one torpedo hit the *Bismarck*'s rudder. She could no longer steer. The mighty *Bismarck* rolled in the waves, unable to move.

The British ships closed in and rained shells and torpedoes against the helpless ship. Finally the *Bismarck* turned over on her side and sank. Most of her crew died with her.

The battleships fought each other like great sea monsters. But there was another kind of battle on the Atlantic. German submarines lay in wait to sink British cargo ships. Small, fast warships called destroyers tried to protect the freighters.

The battle was fought mostly on the cold, stormy North Atlantic Ocean. The crews in the cargo ships knew they risked death if their ships were sunk. And thousands of seamen died. They drowned in the icy waters. They died in explosions. They burned to death as oil in tankers went up in flames. Many drifted for days in lifeboats.

It was a battle England had to win. The freighters carried food, medicines, guns, tanks, and planes. England would starve without the food. She needed the arms to fight Germany. The freighters must reach England.

The cargo ships sailed together in groups called convoys. Most of the ships came from the United States or Canada. Even before the United States was at war with Germany, American destroyers guarded the convoys in the western Atlantic. Late in 1941 the United States and Germany were almost at war.

When war came to the United States on December 7, 1941, the United States was not ready. Its freighters and oil tankers were strung out along the Atlantic coast from Texas to New England. German submarines closed in. Their torpedoes sank ship after ship. Oil from the tankers washed up on miles of beaches from New England to Florida.

German submarines hunted the convoys bound for England. The submarines moved in groups called wolf packs. The British and Americans tried to defend the convoys. But they did not know when the submarines would strike. German submarines were sinking hundreds of freighters. Ships were lost faster than they could be built.

England's supply of food was running low. England's life depended on one thing. Could her navy and airplanes, with American help, fight off the submarines?

A brilliant discovery brought the answer. English sci-

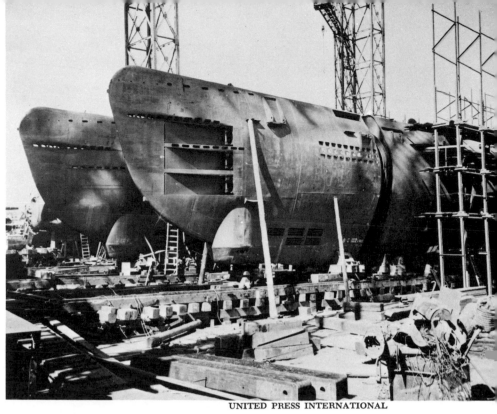

Submarines being assembled in a German shipyard

entists invented a new kind of radar that could detect exactly where the submarines were. Now England needed only one more weapon to destroy the submarines. She needed a way to take a few planes far out to sea to guard the convoys. British shipyards changed big freighters into small aircraft carriers. Destroyers and planes from the carriers closed in on the wolf packs. Submarine after submarine was traced by radar and sunk.

Germany's losses were crippling. Her submarine war could not go on. By the summer of 1943 the long struggle was over.

England had fought off invasion. Britain and the United States together had won the Battle of the Atlantic. Supplies poured into England from the United

States. Ships brought thousands of American soldiers. England was becoming a great stronghold. The Allied armies gathered for a vast effort—the invasion of Hitler's Europe.

But between England and the French coast were the restless, uncertain waters of the English Channel. And across the Channel the German army waited.

7 | Deserts, Seas, and Mountains

Between Europe and Africa lies the Mediterranean Sea. Along its African shore, desert sands stretch for hundreds of miles. Much of the European shore of the Mediterranean is a land of mountains. Italy juts down from Europe into the Mediterranean like a great boot.

Italy wanted to build an empire of her own in the countries along the Mediterranean. Benito Mussolini, dictator of Italy, had declared war on England and France. In September 1940 England had a small army in Egypt. An Italian army attacked the English.

The armies fought on the rock-hard sands of the desert. It was a battle of tanks. Back and forth across the desert sands the tanks moved like ships on a dry sea. At night, miles away from their bases, they steered by the stars, like ships.

The British drove the Italians back. British tanks raced over the desert to cut off the Italian retreat. Thousands of Italian soldiers surrendered, and long lines of prisoners waited, muffled in their overcoats against the winter's cold.

British tanks battle Italian forces on the Egyptian front. The tanks created their own sand cover as they lumbered across the desert.

Hitler was alarmed by the defeat. He knew he and Mussolini must not lose the Mediterranean. Hitler sent his brilliant general Erwin Rommel to the rescue. Rommel brought German troops with him, the proud Afrika Korps, specially trained to fight in the desert. Rommel wasted no time. He made the German and Italian soldiers into a strong fighting army.

Rommel attacked. In a short time the British soldiers were calling him the "Desert Fox." Rommel's men and tanks flowed around the British. They seemed to be everywhere at once. Shells from strong new German guns cut through the armor of British tanks. The English retreated into Egypt. Then the battle came to a halt as both armies waited for their ships to bring them new supplies.

Suddenly it became a war of the sea. German supply convoys moved warily across the Mediterranean. Almost in the center of the Mediterranean lay the rocky British island of Malta. From Malta, British planes and submarines raided the German supply ships. The Germans tried to bomb Malta into ruins, but Malta held firm. The flow of German supplies slowed.

British convoys made the long, dangerous voyage around Africa, then north toward Egypt. The heavy freighters moved slowly in single file through Egypt's Suez Canal, bringing their supplies to a waiting British army.

On the desert the tanks jabbed back and forth at each other. Planes dropped their bombs. But the summer's blistering heat and the insects never waited in the desert war.

"Almost worse than the bombs were the fleas," a British soldier wrote. "How we cursed them on the nights when we hoped to catch an hour's sleep before the night bombers started. The fleas marched up and down our bodies until we thought we would go crazy."

"This sand gets everywhere," another soldier wrote to his family. "My clothes stand up by themselves when I get undressed. Sweat and sand make good concrete."

The armies gathered strength, and once more they struggled back and forth across the desert. By midsummer of 1942 the two armies faced each other near the village of El Alamein, sixty miles from the big Egyptian city of Alexandria. A hundred miles beyond Alexandria was the Suez Canal. If Rommel could win the canal, the Germans would rule the Middle East.

Churchill put a new general in command of the British army. He was General Bernard Montgomery. His

British troops in the Egyptian desert watch as the dump which they set ablaze burns. Nothing of value was left behind for the enemy.

troops soon called him "Monty." Monty worked quickly to train his soldiers better. He gave them faith that they could win. They were proud to call themselves the "Desert Rats."

On a night late in October 1942, Montgomery attacked. A thousand British guns flashed and thundered through the darkness. Montgomery's English and Australian and New Zealand soldiers fought slowly forward through the German minefields. If a soldier or tank touched the ground above a mine that the Germans had buried in the sand, the mine exploded in a deadly blast. Rommel called his minefields his "devil's gardens."

After days of fighting, the British broke through the German defenses. The Germans retreated across the desert. Montgomery and his "Desert Rats" had won the battle of El Alamein. They had saved Egypt and the Middle East.

Far to the west in North Africa a new storm was rising against the German and Italian army. The American and British allies, led by General Dwight Eisenhower, landed armies in French Morocco and Algeria. The French soldiers there did not resist. General Charles de Gaulle of France took command of the French. They called themselves the Free French, and they joined the Allies.

Rommel retreated across the desert to Tunisia. He became ill and could no longer lead his army. Anxiously, Hitler sent a new general and thousands more soldiers to Africa.

The fighting went on for months. A giant vise closed slowly on the Germans. The British and Americans and French came from the west. Montgomery's army came over the desert from the east. The Germans and Italians were pushed back and back. On May 13, 1943, they surrendered.

Germany and Italy had lost the war of the desert and the sea. There was still the war of the mountains.

Hitler's army had swarmed over the countries of Greece and Yugoslavia. Together Germany and Italy controlled the northern shore of the Mediterranean with its mountains and high hills. But the Allies were ready to carry the war to the mountains.

The Allies prepared a vast invasion fleet. Men and tanks and supplies were crowded onto hundreds of ships. The fleet sailed from North Africa, and hours later American and British soldiers stormed ashore on the Italian island of Sicily. Within six weeks they had driven the German and Italian soldiers out of Sicily.

Only the waters of a narrow channel stood between the Allies and Italy itself.

Mussolini's power collapsed, and Italy surrendered. The Germans moved swiftly. They took control of all Italy and braced for an Allied invasion.

The Allies fought their way into Italy at Salerno, south of the big city of Naples. It was a bitter struggle before the Americans and British together gained a foothold on Italian soil.

The Allies moved slowly into the Italian mountains. The Germans had strong defenses. Their main fort was the Roman Catholic monastery of Monte Cassino. It was an ancient building, high on a mountaintop. Its thick stone walls were more than a thousand years old. The Germans set up their guns around the monastery.

For months the Allies tried to capture Monte Cassino. Tanks and trucks could not move up the steep trails. Soldiers toiled up the mountain at night carrying guns and ammunition. The days rang with the sound of gunfire. Gun blasts echoed from rock to rock, like a hundred thunderstorms.

After five long months of fighting, the Allies captured the monastery's ruins. It had been almost four years since Hitler destroyed Poland. Now it was Polish soldiers who entered Monte Cassino first. The Polish flag was raised proudly over one of the German army's strongest forts.

The Germans retreated north through Italy. The Allies entered Rome, Italy's capital, in June 1944. Cheering, shouting, shoving, welcoming crowds lined the streets. The Allied army followed the Germans on northward to a new German defense line far beyond Rome.

It had been a long, bloody battle of the mountains. But Italy had been driven out of the war. The Allies had won a stronghold in Europe itself.

8 | The Rising Storm

The long Russian winter of 1942 dragged on. Finally the summer's sun dried the fields and roads. The German army could move again.

But there was a difference from the summer before. The Russian army had better guns and tanks. Soldiers and officers were better trained. Men from all over Russia had been called into the army. Russia's factories were turning out the supplies of war.

Convoys of British and American ships were also bringing supplies. The convoys sailed to northern Russia through the icy cold seas. They made the long trip to Iran, a country south of Russia. Stalin needed trucks to move his soldiers and supplies quickly. American trucks were sent over the miles of ocean to Iran and driven north into Russia. The power of the Russian army was being massed against the German invader.

Hitler ordered his generals to attack. German troops and tanks rolled across the Russian plains southeast toward the Caucasus Mountains. Beyond the mountains

A German soldier makes his way down a muddy road on the Russian front.

lay Russia's oil fields. "Take the oil fields, and we will cripple Russia," Hitler told his generals.

But Hitler saw a special danger to his plan. To the north of the Caucasus was the big Russian city of Stalingrad on the Volga River. Boats from Stalingrad's docks moved swiftly up and down the river through the heartland of Russia. Stalingrad's radio stations flashed orders and news to Russians fighting the Germans secretly behind the battle lines. Russian troops could move quickly from the city down the Volga or march from there by land to cut off the German army in the Caucasus.

Hitler knew Stalingrad threatened his best hope of defeating Russia. He put General Friedrich von Paulus in command of an army. He gave Paulus his orders, "Destroy Stalingrad."

By August 1942 the German flag flew over the highest mountain in the Caucasus. General Paulus and his army closed in on Stalingrad and drove the Russians back into the city. The Russian army was surrounded except for the river front along the Volga. German bombs and shells blasted the Russians as they tried to bring supplies and soldiers across the mile-wide river.

The Germans hammered at Stalingrad. The city became a battlefield of burned houses and gutted factories. But the Russians fought on.

A new commander, General Vasily Chuikov, came to lead the Russian army. It was night when he made his way across the Volga. Exploding shells flashed light in the blackness as he tried to find his headquarters. Finally a Russian soldier led him along a dark street to a small doorway. The door opened into a trench with a roof of brush and straw, with earth piled on top. Shells were exploding nearby. With each explosion dirt rained down from the roof onto the spread-out maps. General Chuikov had found his headquarters. He took command.

Chuikov rallied his men. He ate and drank and joked with them. He showed them how to fight on Stalingrad's battlefield. "Make every German soldier know that he is living at the end of a Russian gun," he told his soldiers. Night and day his men faced the Germans man to man. The Russians and Germans fought each other building by building, floor by floor, room by room. And still the Russians held the city.

Hitler sent soldiers to Stalingrad from his army in the Caucasus. Gradually he weakened his army there. The drive toward the oil fields had to stop.

The battle at Stalingrad dragged on through the late summer into the cold weather of fall. The Russians still held the city. And help was coming. The Russians massed a new army east of Stalingrad. General Georgi Zhukov was the Russian commander. He had driven the Germans back from Moscow the year before. Now he saved Stalingrad. He sent his army sweeping around the city to surround the Germans.

Hitler's own generals begged him to let the German army fight its way out of the trap. Hitler refused. "Do not give up one foot of ground," he ordered.

The Russians closed the trap. For weeks their shells battered the Germans. They destroyed the Germans' airfield. No supplies could come through. German soldiers were starving and dying. The wounded lay helpless in the cold. General Paulus surrendered what was left of his army.

Now Hitler did not dare leave his soldiers in the Caucasus. He ordered them to retreat. Russia's oil wells were safe. Again the long Russian winter closed in.

Captured German soldiers march through the devastated city of Stalingrad under the control of their Russian captors.

When summer came again, the Germans attacked once more. The war's greatest battle of tanks raged for a week near the Russian city of Kursk. Like dragons, hundreds of tanks raced ahead and wheeled and flowed around each other. Their guns spouted fire. "The earth trembled," an old Russian peasant said. The Russians beat back the attack. The German invasion had been broken.

The Russian army was now far stronger than Germany's. The Russian counterattack began over the long miles of the Russian front. Through the year 1944 the Russians drove steadily westward toward Germany.

A storm was rising over Germany from all sides. In England an army of Allied soldiers was massing. Allied airplanes were pounding Germany's factories and ports and cities with bombs. Each bomber carried gunners to protect it, but the German defense was strong. The gunners faced the swift rush of German fighter planes. Deadly German anti-aircraft shells exploded in puffs of orange flame and black smoke. Thousands of Allied pilots and navigators and gunners were shot down. But day after day the air raids went on, striking at the heart of Germany.

There was another part to the rising storm. This was a secret war by people in the conquered countries.

As the German conquests spread across Europe, the Nazis waged a brutal, cruel fight against helpless people. The dreaded German SS (Security) troops followed the conquering German armies. Hitler ordered the SS to break any resistance against Germany. SS soldiers killed without mercy. They put thousands of people into concentration camps. Strong men and women were sent to work in German factories and on farms.

In every conquered country Hitler lashed out with hatred against one people especially—the Jews. They were treated like animals. They were herded into freight cars and shipped to concentration camps. Thousands died in the camps.

Then Hitler and the Nazi leaders made a brutal decision. All Jews must be killed. Special gas chambers and ovens were built. By the thousands, Jews were gassed to death and their bodies burned. Many people in the conquered countries tried to hide them or to help them escape. But six million innocent Jewish people died.

The Jews were helpless. But there were others in the conquered countries who could fight back. And by the hundreds and thousands they fought.

They were called the resistance or underground fight-

Nazi soldiers perform a brutal execution.

Members of a French resistance patrol in Paris

ers. They were all sorts of people. They could be men or women who farmed the land, or ran railroads, or drove taxicabs, or took care of the sick, or managed businesses, or dug ditches. The Germans did not know who they were. They worked in small groups. Often they did not know each other's names.

The underground fighters fought their war in secret. They were spies. Their hidden radio stations flashed information to Germany's enemies. And they fought the Germans wherever they could. A signal or a whispered order from an underground leader might send a bridge crumbling under a dynamite charge. A factory might flame with a night fire. A lone patrol of German soldiers might fall under a rain of bullets. Capture by the Germans meant torture and death.

The underground soldiers had no uniforms, no bands. But they too were part of the storm that was rising over Germany.

9 | The Beaches of D-Day

By the year 1944 the power of the Allied armies was growing fast. The Russian army was fighting its way from the east toward Germany. To the west the United States and Britain had millions of men in their armies and navies. American factories and shipyards were pouring out the supplies of war and the ships to carry them.

The United States was fighting two wars at once. One war was against Japan thousands of miles away in the Pacific Ocean. The other was the war against Germany across the Atlantic.

Hitler boasted that he had defenses on the Atlantic shore that no enemy could break. But a great army of Americans, British, Canadians, Free French, and Poles waited in England. They were like a giant spring coiled and ready to burst across the English Channel into France.

The American general, Eisenhower, commanded all the Allied armies in the west. Late into the night he studied reports from his officers about plans, special training, and supplies. Orders flashed out from his head-quarters. He worked with his generals to be sure every soldier was trained. The soldiers knew the day of the invasion was coming soon. It was called D-Day. But no one knew when it was to be.

The Allies had built special boats to carry tanks and supplies and men across the Channel. They had floating docks on which to land supplies. The navy and air force were ready to shell and bomb the German defenses.

The Germans knew the attack was coming. But they did not know where. They did not know when.

At last it came to a question of the weather. The tides must be right. The wind must not be high. General Eisenhower studied the weather reports anxiously through the early days of June 1944. His armies were ready, but the weather was uncertain. Then he made the great decision. D-Day would be June 6, 1944. Within a few hours the first waves of Allied troops were on their way across the Channel.

Four thousand ships carrying 175,000 Allied soldiers moved through the darkness toward France. They came out of the dawn mists on D-Day against a line of beaches in French Normandy. The beaches had been given code names—Utah, Omaha, Gold, Juno, and Sword. Thousands of Allied soldiers were dropped from planes to protect both ends of the line of beaches.

Omaha Beach was the hardest to attack. The sea was roughest there. The landing barges, loaded with soldiers, plowed through the waves. Many of the soldiers were seasick. The time came to land. Men and tanks began to pile ashore out of the barges. The Germans opened fire.

Many men never reached the shore. German machine-gun bullets cut them down. German shells ripped into

On the morning of June 6, 1944, General Eisenhower ordered Allied soldiers to land on the beaches of Normandy, France.

the American tanks. But American warships and bombers were blasting at the German defenses. American soldiers and tanks struggled for the shore. Officers and sergeants shouted orders. Men crouched behind what shelter they could find. Their rifles and machine guns sent a rain of bullets against the Germans.

The Americans poured onto the beach. Their tanks charged across the German minefields. American soldiers fought their way through the defenses and the blast of German gunfire. Specially trained soldiers worked to help the wounded.

By nighttime the Americans had fought their way off Omaha Beach. On the beach itself waves washed over wrecked tanks and burned-out trucks and jeeps lying in the shallow water. The beach was cluttered with wasted

Specially trained soldiers help their fellow wounded to safety.

and damaged supplies—barbed wire, food, rifles, telephones, shells, bulldozers, machine guns. Here and there oranges bobbed in the water. The dead lay quiet in the sand.

But the Allies had taken the beaches of Omaha and Utah and Sword and Gold and Juno. Allied soldiers fought their way slowly inland into France.

The fighting raged for weeks as the Allies drove the Germans back. General Montgomery commanded the British troops. General George Patton commanded the Americans. Patton's tanks began to sweep through the German lines. By August, Patton and Montgomery had broken through the German defenses.

Then the Germans suffered a new blow. Allied soldiers from Italy landed in the south of France. They moved north, driving the Germans before them, to join General Patton's army.

The French fought their way on to free Paris. Hitler ordered his commander in Paris to destroy the city. His general refused to obey the order. Paris was saved.

Paris went wild with joy as French and American troops marched through the streets. Young girls rushed to kiss soldiers. People roared their welcome as the Allied soldiers moved on across France and into Belgium. Frenchmen and Belgians were free once more.

The Allies moved swiftly toward Germany. But the Allied supply lines were growing longer. American trucks bounced their way over the rough roads of France to bring gasoline to the Allied tanks and supplies to the armies. The trucks soon had a nickname—the "Red Ball Express."

Hitler fought back desperately. German scientists had invented a new kind of bomb. The bomb's own small jet engine carried it to its target. Hitler launched the new bombs against London. Once more London was under attack. Thousands of buildings were destroyed. Six thousand people died. But the bombs did not save Germany.

Hitler ordered a last desperate attack. Thousands of American soldiers were surrounded at a town named Bastogne, in Belgium. The Germans called on the American general, Anthony McAuliffe, to surrender. He answered with one word: "Nuts." American tanks raced miles and broke through to McAuliffe's men. Hitler's last attack had failed.

The new year 1945 began. The Allies were at the western border of Germany. The Russian army was on Germany's eastern frontier. The Russians had already

The once beautiful city of Nuremberg as it looked when the Germans surrendered in 1945

overrun Rumania, Bulgaria, and much of Hungary. The Americans were moving into the north of Italy. In Yugoslavia resistance fighters under Marshal Tito were freeing their own country. The ring around Nazi Germany had tightened.

Germany grew weaker. There were no more men to draft into the army. American bombers hammered away at the German oil supplies. Gasoline became scarce. Allied bombs were pounding German cities into ruins. The once powerful Luftwaffe was only a shadow.

But Germany still had a strong defense line in the west. The wide Rhine River ran from Switzerland north to the sea. The Allies would have to fight their way across. General Eisenhower prepared for the attack. Hitler ordered all bridges over the Rhine destroyed.

One last bridge remained at a town called Remagen. The Americans captured it before it could be dynamited. American troops poured across the bridge. The drive into Germany had begun.

In America, President Roosevelt was a sick and dying man. But he lived long enough to know that Germany was beaten. He died on April 12, 1945.

President Roosevelt's funeral procession moved solemnly along one of Washington's broad avenues. His coffin, covered by the American flag, was drawn slowly by six white horses. An honor guard of soldiers and sailors marched beside the coffin. Military planes circled overhead. Crowds of people lined the streets. Many of them were weeping. They knew a great leader had died. People around the world mourned him.

Vice-President Harry S Truman became President of the United States.

The day of victory in Europe—V-E Day—was in sight. The end of the war came quickly. The Americans and British moved swiftly into Germany from the west. The Russians invaded from the east. Prisoners of war in Germany were liberated. The pitiful survivors of the concentration camps were freed.

Germany was collapsing into chaos. Soldiers deserted from the army. Desperately, Nazi SS troops turned against deserters. They hung many of them. People looked numbly at the swaying bodies, and walked on. Their first hope was to find food and to live.

Germany was at the mercy of conquering armies. Hitler had boasted of the great German empire. His conquests had ranged thousands of miles. But his dream of empire ended in the ruins of Berlin. The Russians stamped out the final resistance of a little pocket of

Survivors of a Nazi concentration camp cheer their American liberators.

German soldiers at the Berlin zoo. Hitler shot himself in his underground shelter in Berlin. Many Nazi leaders killed themselves. Others struggled to escape.

Germany surrendered. V-E Day came at last on May 8, 1945. The Allies had won the war in Europe.

10 | The Guns Fall Silent

Japanese planes had swarmed over Pearl Harbor on December 7, 1941. In the months that followed, Japan won a rich empire. Her army took the coastlands of China. Her ships and troops and planes moved swiftly southward from Japan. Within months the Japanese flag waved in victory over hundreds of Pacific Ocean islands and all the lands of southeast Asia. The United States and England and Holland had been driven out of most of the western Pacific. Only Australia remained as an Allied base.

Admiral Isoroku Yamamoto, the commander of the Japanese navy, knew that his navy was far stronger than the Americans'. He made his plans to destroy the rest of the United States fleet in the Pacific.

Admiral Chester Nimitz commanded what remained of the American fleet at Pearl Harbor. He was sure the Japanese would attack again. He had only a few ships, and he knew he had almost no time to get ready. Engineers told him they needed three weeks to repair the

American planes dropped the first atomic bomb on Hiroshima in August 1945. Smoke rose 20,000 feet above the Japanese city.

damaged aircraft carrier *Yorktown*. "I will give you three days," the Admiral said. In three days the *Yorktown* was ready to go to sea.

Yamamoto sailed from Japan with a powerful fleet of warships. There were eight aircraft carriers in the fleet. Four were large. Nimitz had only three carriers—the *Yorktown* and *Enterprise,* and the smaller *Hornet.*

But Admiral Nimitz had one great advantage. His men had discovered the secret of the Japanese radio code. This was the special language Admiral Yamamoto used to send his orders to his ships. When Nimitz knew the code, he knew exactly what Yamamoto was planning to do. He learned the Japanese would make a surprise attack first against the island of Midway. Midway was the western gate to Hawaii and Pearl Harbor. The American carriers sailed from Pearl Harbor. Only a few officers knew Admiral Nimitz's plan. Secretly the carriers moved near Midway.

Early on the morning of June 4, 1942, a wave of Japanese planes stormed over Midway. They dropped their bombs and flew back to their carriers to refuel and re-arm. Planes from the *Yorktown* and *Enterprise* and *Hornet* swooped down on the Japanese carriers. Within five minutes they sank all four of Japan's big carriers. Three hundred and thirty Japanese planes sank with them.

In those five minutes Japan's navy had been badly damaged. The rest of the Japanese fleet sailed for home.

Late in the summer of 1942 the United States army and navy started on the long road to Japan. American and Australian troops under General MacArthur attacked the Japanese on the huge island of New Guinea, north of Australia. American marines landed on Guadalcanal, an island northeast of Australia.

From a distance, the white beaches of the islands looked like a tropical heaven. Palm trees waved in the soft breezes. But the soldiers and marines soon learned it was no heaven. Rains poured down. The jungle steamed in the heat. The men swatted at mosquitoes. All kinds of bugs flew and crawled and bit. Rats raided the food. Many of the men fell sick with malaria and jungle fever. Swamp water soaked clothing and rotted it away.

One day in the long fight for New Guinea a small group of American soldiers was holding a dangerous outpost. It was important to keep it. The general in command made his way to them. "What do you need?" he demanded. One soldier gave the answer. He flipped into a half somersault and held it. The seat of his pants had rotted out. "For God's sake, General, pants!"

Fighting raged on the two islands. Japanese soldiers came screaming out of the jungle to attack. The navies fought to control the seas off Guadalcanal. Ship after ship was sunk. The marines nicknamed the water "Iron Bottom Sound." At last the Japanese were driven off Guadalcanal. Guadalcanal was American. The first step had been taken on the long march toward Japan.

Japan herself was a great fortress. Thousands of miles of ocean and hundreds of fortified islands guarded her. But American power was growing fast. Shipyards and factories in the United States clanged with noise as men and women worked day and night. A flow of ships and men and planes and submarines moved across the Pacific.

American sailors and airmen fought the Japanese over hundreds of miles of ocean. American marines and soldiers scrambled ashore on the islands. They ran for cover across the beaches in a hail of Japanese bullets. The islands' palm trees stood tall and stiff, tattered by bombs and shells. The Japanese fought back savagely from their defenses. They hid in the jungle. They dug into the hills. They holed up in caves. They fought to their death. They would not surrender.

Most Americans did not know the faraway Pacific Ocean islands where their men were fighting. They heard on their radios the strange names of the islands— Tarawa, Kwajalein, Eniwetok, Saipan, Peleliu. But Americans knew their men were moving closer to Japan.

The United States navy was fighting another kind of war beneath the sea. The navy's submarines moved silently under the water. Japan's ships had to sail thousands of miles from Japan to the farthest lands she had conquered. American submarines lay in wait. Their torpedoes streaked through the water. Japanese warships and cargo ships went to the bottom of the ocean. The Japanese supply lines were breaking.

By 1944 the American drive was moving faster and faster. In October the Americans reached the Philippines—the gateway to Japan. General MacArthur had kept his promise to return.

The Japanese saw a chance to trap MacArthur's men once again on the Philippines. MacArthur was landing his army on the Philippine island of Leyte. Three Japanese fleets attacked. American warships were on guard. The fleets battled each other over hundreds of miles. At one point only a few American destroyers and a group of small, slow aircraft carriers stood between a strong Japanese fleet and MacArthur's men on the beach. The American destroyer *Johnston* was nearest the enemy.

The captain of the *Johnston* was Commander Ernest

Marines aboard a navy carrier watch columns of smoke rise from the shores of Leyte.

E. Evans. He was a Cherokee Indian, and a hard fighter. When he took command of the *Johnston,* he told his men, "This is going to be a fighting ship. Anyone who doesn't want to go along had better get off right now."

Evans moved quickly to draw the enemy's gunfire away from the aircraft carriers. He sank a big Japanese cruiser. He attacked another cruiser. Japanese gunfire knocked out the *Johnston's* engines. Fire raged through the ship. Commander Evans fought on. Finally the *Johnston* sank. With her went her captain and half of her crew. But the *Johnston* and other destroyers had saved most of the carriers. They had protected MacArthur's troops on the island of Leyte.

The battles were a great victory for the United States. One Japanese fleet was sunk. The power of the Japanese

navy was broken. MacArthur's army went on to free the
Philippines.

The ring of American power was closing on Japan.
Army planes flew across the high mountains between
India and China to bring supplies to the Chinese armies.
The British pressed from India to free Burma and to
reopen a road to China. The army air force flew their
huge bombers, the B-29s, against Japan. Thousands died
in Tokyo and other Japanese cities as the bombs sent
fire racing through the wooden buildings.

Japan had still one more weapon to use against the
Americans. The weapon was her suicide planes—the
kamikazes. There was a Japanese story that long ago a
great wind had blown a fleet of enemy ships away from
Japan. The Japanese had called the wind "kamikaze"—
the divine wind. Now they gave the name to their suicide planes. Pilots of the kamikazes volunteered to fly
their planes and crash them into American ships. Each
plane carried a bomb. There was no return for the pilots
—only death.

American anti-aircraft gunners fought desperately to
shoot down the Japanese pilots. But the kamikazes took
a terrible toll of American ships and men.

Two more islands stood in the way before the Americans could invade the home islands of Japan. One was
the small, rocky island of Iwo Jima. The other was Okinawa, near the coast of Japan. The battle for the islands
was a bloody struggle. More than a hundred thousand
Japanese soldiers died on Okinawa. They would not surrender. Nor did their general. He put on his full-dress
uniform and knelt down. In an age-old Japanese ritual
he killed himself.

Okinawa and Iwo Jima were in American hands. The

Japanese empire was collapsing. Her fleet and air force were almost gone. American army bombers were hammering Japanese cities into burning ruins. Food was running low. Russia was preparing to declare war against Japan. The American army was massing troops and ships and planes—ready to invade Japan itself.

Sitting at his desk in the White House, President Truman had a fateful decision to make. Hundreds of thousands of lives were at stake whatever he decided. He knew that in years to come the world would judge him by what he did. But he was certain that a million Americans and Japanese would die if America had to invade Japan. He made his decision. He would use the most terrible weapon the world had ever yet seen—the atomic bomb that American scientists had perfected only weeks before.

On the morning of August 6, 1945, a B-29 bomber, named *Enola Gay* by its crew, flew over the Japanese city of Hiroshima. It was 8:15 in the morning. The bomb struck. A flash like the light of the sun blasted over the city. People, factories, houses, walls, railroad trains vanished into dust. A whirlwind of air carried the white-hot dust far above the ruined city. People died by the thousands. Farther from the center of the bomb's explosion houses collapsed like cardboard. Fires broke out. People died, trapped in the wreckage of their homes.

Three days later another atomic bomb was dropped on the city of Nagasaki.

The Supreme War Council of Japan met in the presence of Emperor Hirohito. For a long time the Council argued about what Japan must do. Finally Premier Kantaro Suzuki stood up. "Gentlemen," he said, "we have not agreed. We have no time left. I will seek the Em-

Two Japanese walk through the ruins of Hiroshima.

peror's guidance." He waited before the imperial throne.

Emperor Hirohito spoke. Japan surrendered.

Japan's surrender message reached President Truman late in the afternoon of August 14, 1945. At seven o'clock that evening he announced the news to reporters. A roar of cheers rocked the room. The reporters rushed to telephone their newspapers and radio stations, and the news flashed around the world.

All through the evening and on through the night, across the United States, crowds went wild. City streets were jammed with laughing, shouting people. Strangers hugged each other. Sailors kissed pretty girls. Automobile horns, church bells, factory whistles sounded the happy cry of victory. It was every American's own V-J Day, the day of victory over Japan.

photos from WIDE WORLD PHOTOS

Above, President Truman announces news of the Japanese surrender to reporters at the White House in August 1945. *Below,*
a crowd in New York's Times Square rejoices over the surrender.

The Allies receive Japan's formal surrender aboard the *Missouri*. General Douglas MacArthur (*far left*) looks on.

On September 2, 1945, the Allies received Japan's formal surrender on the deck of the battleship *Missouri* in Tokyo Bay. It was six years since Hitler had struck at Poland and World War II had begun. Millions of men and women and children had died. Millions more had suffered cruelly.

At last the guns had fallen silent.

Index

Italic number indicates photograph